DECLUTTER LIKE A MOTHER PLANNER

ALLIE CASAZZA

NELSON
BOOKS
An Imprint of Thomas Nelson

Declutter Like a Mother Planner

© 2021, 2023 Allie Casazza

Published in Nashville, Tennessee, by Nelson Books, an imprint of Thomas Nelson. Nelson Books and Thomas Nelson are registered trademarks of HarperCollins Christian Publishing, Inc.

Published in association with literary agent Jenni Burke of Illuminate Literary Agency, www.illuminateliterary.com.

Thomas Nelson titles may be purchased in bulk for educational, business, fundraising, or sales promotional use. For information, please e-mail SpecialMarkets@ThomasNelson.com.

Scripture quotations are taken from the Revised Standard Version of the Bible. Copyright © 1946, 1952, and 1971 National Council of the Churches of Christ in the United States of America. Used by permission. All rights reserved worldwide.

Any internet addresses, phone numbers, or company or product information printed in this book are offered as a resource and are not intended in any way to be or to imply an endorsement by Thomas Nelson, nor does Thomas Nelson vouch for the existence, content, or services of these sites, phone numbers, companies, or products beyond the life of this book.

Painted Cover: Laci Fowler (@lacifowlerart)

Interior design: Kristy Edwards

Printed in China

23 24 25 26 27   DSC   10 9 8 7 6 5 4 3 2 1

INTRODUCTION

OUR HOMES ARE OVERFLOWING WITH STUFF AND WE'RE DROWNING with no lifeline in sight. We keep thinking our possessions will make us happy, so we keep collecting more. But they're not making us happy; they're weighing us down, pulling us under. Our overabundance is affecting us negatively. And not just us, but our families too. Our physical health, our mental health, our relationships are all suffering because we have *too much stuff*.

Modern research studies show a direct link between the amount of physical possessions in a house and the stress level of the female homeowner. One study done at UCLA found that the more stuff there was in a woman's house, the higher her level of stress hormones. This same study also found that women subconsciously relate how happy they are with their families and home lives to how they feel about their homes. So, the more clutter and chaos in her home, the less happy a woman is with her family and her life.[1]

Our stuff is literally stealing from us. It's stealing the most precious thing in the world: life. Marshall Goldsmith wrote in his book *Triggers*, "If we do not create and control our environment, our environment creates and controls us."[2] We need to take control back. We need to set our homes up to reflect our values, so our homes are not constantly pulling us away from what's most important.

That's what moms need more than anything else. The type of minimalism that means less cleaning, less stress, less distraction from the people they most care about—and more energy and free time to focus on their priorities. They want to feel the joy of always being ready for company to drop by without stress, worry, or embarrassment. They want to enjoy their home rather than be owned by it. They want to be the mom who plays rather than the mom who's always cleaning up. They want to be a happier person.

Over the next twelve months, I will guide you through decluttering. Each month I'll equip you with content to educate you on decluttering your home, how minimalism can steal your joy, and how to change your life with this new lifestyle. Each month includes a monthly overview, weekly overviews, and fillable lists to help you adopt a decluttered life and truly shift your mindset. To help you stay motivated and encouraged, there's a monthly podcast recommendation of The Purpose Show—just scan the QR code.

If you want to skip ahead, it's totally your choice. Declutter and grow at your own pace. If you do skip ahead, you can still use this planner, and use the lists and content to check in and stick to your goals.

I see you, I love you, and I'm for you!

ROOTING FOR YOU ALWAYS,

Allie

MONTH

goals

TO DO LIST

- ◇
- ◇
- ◇
- ◇
- ◇
- ◇
- ◇
- ◇
- ◇
- ◇
- ◇

BIRTHDAYS

IMPORTANT DATES

reminders

WHAT'S SUPPORTING ME

WHAT'S NOT SUPPORTING ME

PRIORITIZE YOUR LIFE

I DON'T CARE ABOUT THE RULES. I DON'T CARE HOW OTHER PEOPLE define minimalism. I really don't even care about minimalism itself. For me, it's simply a means to get to the goal of a better, lighter life. I'm definitely not interested in the one-size-fits-all approach to minimalism that has taken the world by storm the past few years. You know the kind I'm talking about. It's the kind that only works if you're single or bored or don't have kids.

I don't care if you call what I do minimalism. I'm using that word because that's what everyone else calls the removal of excess stuff. I needed a well-known word to express what it was that took me from feeling overwhelmed, depressed, overcomplicated, and overburdened to feeling light, joyful, present, and purposeful in my life. But maybe the word I'm looking for is *less*. Maybe it's *simplicity*. Maybe it's *intentionality*. Or maybe I need to make up my own word. How about *simplicitism*? That feels a bit better, but it's a mouthful. And it's not really a word, but it's fine.

Whatever we call it, it's about being intentional. It's about simplifying. It's about having less of what doesn't matter in order to make room for what does.

So, what kind of minimalism do moms need? *Moms need the kind of minimalism that works for them.*

Take a second to let the simplicity of that sink in. The kind of minimalism moms need is the kind that works for moms. It's the kind that helps you, the kind that supports you, the kind that makes you feel lighter without making you feel like there's a massive set of unrealistic rules you need to follow. It's the kind of minimalism that is relative to the family you're raising, the home you live in, the climate in your region, whether you live in a suburb or a city, and most importantly, the story you're telling with your life and home.

Your home is a reflection of your life's story. If the minimalism you're implementing isn't relative to the story you're telling, you're going to end up getting rid of stuff just for the sake of having less. This kind of rigid, rules-based minimalism can end up being the opposite of freeing. It can leave you obsessing over the number of things you have in your home rather than creating space for life to happen and actually resting in the enjoyment of it.

That being said, you obviously don't need to keep every single thing in your house. That also wouldn't support you in being present for your life. Minimalism that works is all about balance. Most of the time, things are just things, but we over-complicate them by attaching meaning to objects. Here's the foundation I need you to understand: what takes up your space takes up your time.

Let's use a basic household appliance to demonstrate my point. I'm going to go with the toaster. Whether you have a toaster or a toaster oven, it's safe to assume you probably have some sort of bread-crisping apparatus in your home. Don't get hung up on the appliance, insert whatever you have in your kitchen and just work with me.

Your toaster sits on your kitchen counter waiting to be used. It doesn't seem like it requires very much of you, and it doesn't even take up that much space. But because it's there, you use it. It requires you to empty out the crumb tray, wipe it down, and clean around it or pick it up to clean underneath it (on the days you care enough to do so). Even something as inconspicuous as a toaster that just sits there takes up your time every so often.

Let's estimate that it takes about two seconds to put the bread in the toaster and push the handle down, and then two more seconds to turn it off and get the bread out. Let's say that it takes about ten seconds to dump out the crumb tray and wipe it down, and then ten more seconds to clean the front of the toaster. Let's add ten more seconds for a once-per-week, deep-cleaning day where you wipe the counter under the toaster and make it shiny. That's approximately 178 seconds a week.

That's 9,256 seconds a year.

That's over 154 minutes a year.

That's over 2.5 hours a year spent *on your freakin' toaster.*

Now, think about every single thing in your house. Think about every sock, every shoe, every photograph, every piece of decor, every notepad, every bobby pin, every piece of paper, every board game, every cord, every toy . . . every single thing taking up some amount of your time.

This. Adds. Up.

Do you see my point? Every single thing that takes up space in your home is also taking up some amount of your time. Let this be a reminder that you're not a failure at this. You're overwhelmed because this is *a lot*.

If we want change, we need to face the things that are holding us back. We often overcomplicate our lives by overstuffing our homes and making our lives harder than they need to be. We give our time to things that don't ultimately matter, and then complain that there isn't enough time in the day.

Getting clutter out of your way is something that will help you. Whatever your situation and your reasons, minimalism is whatever you need it to be as long as you're asking this question: Is this aligning with the life I want to live?

What I want is for you to make a version of minimalism (or simplicitism or whatever you need to call it) that is unique to you and your family. I want to give you the gift of *less of what doesn't matter* for the sake of *more of what does matter*. Start by asking yourself: Is my house working for me or against me? If you feel as though your house is working against you, it is not supporting you, which is the opposite of what it is meant to do.

If you start to feel overwhelmed while trying to climb out of the overwhelm, I want you to picture what you're working toward. If you get stuck in the details and sorting through a room of your house feels like too much, like you're stuck in the muck with no end in sight, I want you to know that there *is* an end, and it is not far away.

So, let's jump into the future and imagine a few scenarios.

SCENARIO 1: You come home at the end of a long day with your arms full of groceries. You open the door and immediately feel at peace. Your home is restful. It's nice. It's welcoming. It's just what you need after a long day of getting stuff done. You're not wading through a mess and envisioning an endless list of chores in your head. Nope! Your task list is checked off for the day. It's time to put the groceries away in a kitchen you feel good in, make dinner, relax, and enjoy your family.

SCENARIO 2: Dinner is finished, the kids had their baths and are in bed, and it's time for you to start your end-of-the-day routine. Instead of running around the house overwhelmed by the mess left over from the day and trying to clean every single surface so you can have some semblance of peace before you crash into bed, you calmly walk through your house, picking up a few things here and there. You wipe down the kitchen counters, put a small load of folded laundry in the dresser, toss a pair of dirty socks in the hamper. It takes you twenty minutes, and then you're able to sit down with a glass of wine or a cup of tea and breathe. You can relax because everything is done, and it didn't take hours.

SCENARIO 3: You wake up in the morning, open your eyes, and the first thing you see is a neat room. A relaxing haven. You get ready in a bathroom that's functional and tidy. You walk downstairs and make breakfast in a clean and organized kitchen. Your day automatically starts with good energy, not stress. Your phone alerts you to a text message from your mother-in-law saying she's going to drop by real quick to bring you something. Instead of feeling panicked and shoveling things behind the shower curtain (that was always my go-to hiding spot), you're ready. Your house is lived-in and normal. Sure, there are shoes by the front door, cords coming out from the TV cabinet, and a few scattered things here and there (because, hey, people live here), but it's not a mess. There is nothing for you to freak out about. Your home is easy to run. Everything has a place. You're not constantly cleaning because the clutter is gone and it's not possible for your home to get *that* chaotic. Less than an hour a day is all you need to keep your home clean.

I know this may be *so far* from your reality. I get it. But I don't want you to buy into the belief that none of this is possible. That's not true. I'm going to help you make this a reality over the course of this planner.

You are in charge of your life. You don't have to play the victim one second longer. I'm not saying things haven't been hard for you. I'm not belittling any of the experiences that led you here. But from this point forward, you get to make the decision for how you want your life to go. You get to set yourself—and your home—free.

LISTEN TO THE PURPOSE SHOW

Stress Is a Choice

Episode 262

MON	◯	TUE	◯	WED	◯

MON	◯	TUE	◯	WED	◯

MON	◯	TUE	◯	WED	◯

MON	◯	TUE	◯	WED	◯

MON	◯	TUE	◯	WED	◯

MONTH ....

THUR ◯	FRI ◯	SAT ◯	SUN ◯
THUR ◯	FRI ◯	SAT ◯	SUN ◯
THUR ◯	FRI ◯	SAT ◯	SUN ◯
THUR ◯	FRI ◯	SAT ◯	SUN ◯
THUR ◯	FRI ◯	SAT ◯	SUN ◯

MONDAY

....

....

....

....

....

....

◇ ....

◇ ....

◇ ....

◇ ....

◇ ....

◇ ....

TUESDAY

....

....

....

....

....

....

◇ ....

◇ ....

◇ ....

◇ ....

◇ ....

◇ ....

WEDNESDAY

....

....

....

....

....

....

◇ ....

◇ ....

◇ ....

◇ ....

◇ ....

◇ ....

◇ ....

THURSDAY

FRIDAY

SATURDAY

SUNDAY

MONDAY

....

....

....

....

....

....

◇ ....

◇ ....

◇ ....

◇ ....

◇ ....

◇ ....

TUESDAY

....

....

....

....

....

....

◇ ....

◇ ....

◇ ....

◇ ....

◇ ....

◇ ....

WEDNESDAY

....

....

....

....

....

....

◇ ....

◇ ....

◇ ....

◇ ....

◇ ....

◇ ....

◇ ....

THURSDAY

◇ ....

◇ ....

....

◇ ....

....

◇ ....

....

◇ ....

....

◇ ....

....

◇ ....

....

◇ ....

FRIDAY

◇ ....

....

◇ ....

....

◇ ....

....

◇ ....

....

◇ ....

....

◇ ....

....

◇ ....

SATURDAY

....

....

....

◇ ....

◇ ....

SUNDAY

....

....

....

◇ ....

◇ ....

MONDAY

....

....

....

....

....

....

◇ ....

◇ ....

◇ ....

◇ ....

◇ ....

◇ ....

TUESDAY

....

....

....

....

....

....

◇ ....

◇ ....

◇ ....

◇ ....

◇ ....

◇ ....

WEDNESDAY

....

....

....

....

....

....

◇ ....

◇ ....

◇ ....

◇ ....

◇ ....

◇ ....

◇ ....

THURSDAY

....

....

....

....

....

◇ ....

◇ ....

◇ ....

◇ ....

◇ ....

◇ ....

◇ ....

FRIDAY

....

....

....

....

....

◇ ....

◇ ....

◇ ....

◇ ....

◇ ....

◇ ....

◇ ....

SATURDAY

....

....

◇ ....

◇ ....

SUNDAY

....

....

◇ ....

◇ ....

MONDAY

....

....

....

....

....

◇ ....

◇ ....

◇ ....

◇ ....

◇ ....

◇ ....

TUESDAY

....

....

....

....

....

◇ ....

◇ ....

◇ ....

◇ ....

◇ ....

◇ ....

WEDNESDAY

....

....

....

....

....

◇ ....

◇ ....

◇ ....

◇ ....

◇ ....

◇ ....

◇ ....

THURSDAY

◇
◇
◇
◇
◇
◇
◇

FRIDAY

◇
◇
◇
◇
◇
◇
◇

SATURDAY

◇
◇

SUNDAY

◇
◇

CLUTTER IS

A THIEF

MONTH

goals

TO DO LIST

◇ _____
◇ _____
◇ _____
◇ _____
◇ _____
◇ _____
◇ _____
◇ _____
◇ _____
◇ _____
◇ _____

BIRTHDAYS

_____
_____
_____
_____
_____

IMPORTANT DATES

_____
_____
_____
_____

reminders

PROGRESS NOT PERFECTION

PROGRESS NOT PERFECTION

CLUTTER IS A THIEF

HERE'S WHAT YOU NEED TO KNOW BEFORE WE START: THIS PLANNER is based on my annual Declutter Like a Mother® (DLAM) challenge. In this challenge, our mantra is *progress not perfection*. Because here's the thing, there are already so many different voices telling you how to do all the nitty-gritty details of every single thing in your house and exactly how you should have everything set up. But if those well-intentioned opinions have not been serving you, it's time to let me help.

My approach is to help you create real, lasting progress the simplest way possible. Progress that is actually going to put a dent in the chaos and stress you have been handling for far too long. And girl, that is not going to happen by hyper-focusing on how your closet is organized or what the inside of your refrigerator looks like, but rather by working through mental blocks and shifting your thinking about the way your home and life should work, and then using those mental shifts to physically remove the junk without crazy amounts of fear. We're going to go through the main areas of your home and radically purge them, so you *feel* the progress and *see* the results in your family and home.

Let me add here: this whole process has nothing to do with whether you are a naturally neat or messy person. This is not about being tidy or "getting organized." This is about taking your *space* back. It's about taking your *time* back. It's about getting the unnecessary crap out of the way and unclogging your mind.

This is a method that will clear that stuck, stagnant energy in your home that comes from having too much stuff. Being neat or messy has nothing to do with it. You can be a naturally messy person (that's me!) and have an uncluttered space. Clutter does not equal messy. Clutter equals clutter, and it's hurting you regardless of whether you're messy or tidy by nature.

Look at your calendar now and decide when you will do your decluttering. Will you do it for hours at a time? Will you break it up into ten-minute chunks? It doesn't matter. All that matters is making the time and following through. You can do it early before your kids wake up, on your lunch break, after you put your kids to bed, during nap time, on the weekend, whatever fits best (not easiest—best). However,

I want to warn you of the temptation to do more and work longer, especially in the beginning when you're all inspired, full of momentum, and totally on a roll. Be careful not to run yourself into the ground! Don't derail your efforts by burning out too soon. Pace yourself. You've likely accumulated a lot of stuff over a lot of years. It's okay for this to take some time. The point is to find something that works for you and make slow, steady progress.

The key to succeeding is this: prioritize your life. This isn't extra. This doesn't fall into the "would be nice" category on your to-do list. This is important and it matters. Find the time and get it done, so you can literally create more time for what matters in your life. Show up for yourself and your family.

Maybe you'll have to make a sacrifice somewhere to fit this into your day. Do it. The return on investment is huge, because every time you finish a decluttering session, you'll have given yourself back minutes of the day that you didn't previously have. Remember, what takes up your space takes up your time.

Also remember that this is only temporary. You don't have to make the sacrifice forever. Just long enough to simplify your home, lighten your load, and make your life a whole lot better.

WHAT TO EXPECT

Let me toss you a pro tip: don't go into a room, gut it, throw everything on the floor, then start making decisions and sorting things into piles. All that's gonna do is overwhelm you even more and have you abandoning rooms with piles everywhere. What I want you to do in each room is simply pick up the first thing you see, look at it, and make a decision. Decide first, then put that item into a pile on the floor. This will keep you from pulling out everything you own and getting that "project overwhelm WTF did I do" feeling.

You should have three piles: keep, toss, and donate. That's it.

Now, I'm going to be honest with you. You're going to come across things that you'll feel incapable of making decisions about. The tiny white dress your daughter wore home from the hospital or the handmade quilt your grandmother gave you right before she passed away—you'll hold those items in your hands and feel totally stuck.

It's okay to feel overwhelmed by the decision-making process, but don't let it keep you from making progress. When you find yourself stuck on something sentimental or difficult, just set it aside or put it back for now. You'll have to deal with it eventually (I address it later, and you'll be a total pro by then!), but you don't need to deal with it in the middle of a productive purging session.

I strongly encourage you *not* to put away your "keep" pile until you're done with the room you're currently working on. The name of the game is short spurts of massive progress in one area at a time!

When you're done with a room, *follow through with your piles*. You are not done with a decluttering session until you have followed it all the way through! Everything in your "keep" pile needs to be put in its new home. Everything in your "trash" pile needs to be bagged up and carried out to the garbage can. Everything in your "donate" pile needs to be bagged up and put in the back of your car for a trip to the donation center. Once these things are done, you can check the box on your purge session for the day.

THE ACTUAL CLUTTER

One thing I know for sure is that clutter is much more than piles of hidden stuff you probably don't need. Clutter is a thief. It steals the space you're paying for, it steals your time, it steals your energy, it steals your mental clarity, it steals your joy. I've seen it straight up steal people's quality of life. On the surface, this all sounds pretty dramatic. But it's the truth. I've seen it over and over again, in my own life and in others'.

Here's the problem: most people's homes are working against them because of how they have them set up. They move into their homes, put a million appliances in the kitchen, put clothes they hate or don't wear in the closets, put books they'll never read on the shelves—they have too much stuff. So they stack boxes in the garage or in the attic and throw knickknacks and odds and ends on the tops of dressers. The dining tables are no longer used for eating together as a family, but for spaces where they throw the stuff they don't know what to do with. They eat at the kitchen counter instead, which is littered with bills, school paperwork, and junk mail.

Sound familiar? If so, is that what you want? Is that the house you want to live in? Your home is supposed to be a safe space where memories are made. It's supposed to be a haven, a place where you can rest, recharge, be productive, and live well. Is your home set up in a way that makes this possible or makes this harder? Is your home a time and energy suck because of the layers of stuff you have to maintain?

We have too much of everything because we're afraid to make the decision to let go of anything. It all comes down to fear. Every single thing. Every single time. We don't want to let go of our stuff because we spent money on it (or someone else did), and we're afraid we'll feel guilty, or worse, selfish!

When we say yes to keeping our junk, we're saying no to feeling peace in our own homes. When we say yes to constantly having to clean and maintain, we're saying no to doing something purposeful or enjoyable. You don't have to keep saying yes to the things that aren't serving you. You don't have to drown in your stuff.

This passes on to generations still to come. I don't want my death to come with the added burden for my kids to have to sort through rooms and layers and drawers and boxes full of stuff no one needs. I don't want my kids to take time out of their lives to sort through what I avoided while also grieving.

This is a gift you give your family. This shifts the legacy you leave behind. This matters. Status quo isn't good enough for your family. Let's move beyond it.

LISTEN TO THE PURPOSE SHOW

Declutter 101: Where Do I Start?

Episode 103

MON	TUE	WED

MON	TUE	WED

MON	TUE	WED

MON	TUE	WED

MON	TUE	WED

M O N T H ....

THUR ◯	FRI ◯	SAT ◯	SUN ◯
THUR ◯	FRI ◯	SAT ◯	SUN ◯
THUR ◯	FRI ◯	SAT ◯	SUN ◯
THUR ◯	FRI ◯	SAT ◯	SUN ◯
THUR ◯	FRI ◯	SAT ◯	SUN ◯

MONDAY

....

....

....

....

....

....

◇ ....

◇ ....

◇ ....

◇ ....

◇ ....

◇ ....

TUESDAY

....

....

....

....

....

....

◇ ....

◇ ....

◇ ....

◇ ....

◇ ....

◇ ....

WEDNESDAY

....

....

....

....

....

....

◇ ....

◇ ....

◇ ....

◇ ....

◇ ....

◇ ....

◇ ....

THURSDAY

◇ ....
◇ ....
◇ ....
◇ ....
◇ ....
◇ ....
◇ ....

FRIDAY

◇ ....
◇ ....
◇ ....
◇ ....
◇ ....
◇ ....
◇ ....

SATURDAY

SUNDAY

◇ ....
◇ ....

MONDAY

....

....

....

....

....

....

◇ ....

◇ ....

◇ ....

◇ ....

◇ ....

◇ ....

TUESDAY

....

....

....

....

....

....

◇ ....

◇ ....

◇ ....

◇ ....

◇ ....

◇ ....

WEDNESDAY

....

....

....

....

....

....

◇ ....

◇ ....

◇ ....

◇ ....

◇ ....

◇ ....

◇ ....

THURSDAY

◇ ....

◇ ....

◇ ....

◇ ....

◇ ....

◇ ....

◇ ....

FRIDAY

◇ ....

◇ ....

◇ ....

◇ ....

◇ ....

◇ ....

◇ ....

SATURDAY

◇ ....

◇ ....

SUNDAY

◇ ....

◇ ....

MONDAY

◇ ....

◇ ....

◇ ....

◇ ....

◇ ....

◇ ....

TUESDAY

◇ ....

◇ ....

◇ ....

◇ ....

◇ ....

◇ ....

WEDNESDAY

◇ ....

◇ ....

◇ ....

◇ ....

◇ ....

◇ ....

◇ ....

THURSDAY

◇ ....

◇ ....

◇ ....

◇ ....

◇ ....

◇ ....

◇ ....

FRIDAY

◇ ....

◇ ....

◇ ....

◇ ....

◇ ....

◇ ....

◇ ....

SATURDAY

◇ ....

◇ ....

SUNDAY

◇ ....

◇ ....

MONDAY

◇

◇

◇

◇

◇

◇

TUESDAY

◇

◇

◇

◇

◇

◇

WEDNESDAY

◇

◇

◇

◇

◇

◇

◇

THURSDAY

◇ ....
◇ ....
◇ ....
◇ ....
◇ ....
◇ ....
◇ ....

FRIDAY

◇ ....
◇ ....
◇ ....
◇ ....
◇ ....
◇ ....
◇ ....

SATURDAY

◇ ....
◇ ....

SUNDAY

◇ ....
◇ ....

MONTH

goals

TO DO LIST

- ◇ _____
- ◇ _____
- ◇ _____
- ◇ _____
- ◇ _____
- ◇ _____
- ◇ _____
- ◇ _____
- ◇ _____
- ◇ _____
- ◇ _____

BIRTHDAYS

_____

_____

_____

_____

_____

IMPORTANT DATES

_____

_____

_____

_____

reminders

AFFIRMATIONS TO STAY MOTIVATED

AFFIRMATIONS TO STAY MOTIVATED

DITCH STEREOTYPICAL MINIMALISM

WHAT WE'RE DOING HERE IS CREATING A SPACE THAT ALIGNS WITH how you want to feel in your home. But if you're not careful, you can fall into soul-sucking minimalism traps.

Instead of giving you the joy and freedom that you so desperately desire, this lifestyle of minimalism that seems like an oasis can turn into quicksand fast. I can't tell you how many times I've seen trendy, stereotypical minimalism suck the joy right out of people's lives. They give up their decision-making power and get lost in a life of counting and rule-following—counting jeans, counting shoes, counting books. Life becomes all about keeping the amount of possessions they own under a certain number. It becomes about following the rules some minimalist teacher somewhere told them they had to follow in order to be a "minimalist."

These people are missing the point of simplifying by obsessing over the details and the numbers. It's *so easy* to do. They're exchanging the handcuffs their stuff shackled them with for a new set of shiny handcuffs gifted to them by "minimalist rules." They're still giving power and energy to their stuff—in a new way.

SIGNS YOU'RE LETTING MINIMALISM STEAL YOUR JOY

1. You find yourself stalling and procrastinating instead of taking action because you're afraid you'll "do it wrong."
2. You maybe, sort of, but definitely obsess over how somebody else does this.
3. You look for a way this won't work for you, instead of being open-minded and willing to give it a try.
4. You feel guilty keeping things you love. You always feel like you could, and should, get rid of more.
5. You expect decluttering to be a one-and-done event instead of a process.

6. You feel guilt over the amount of money you've wasted on your stuff, instead of letting the realization make you a more mindful consumer.
7. You believe you can never shop or purchase anything again.

So, don't obsess over the rules, or the details, or the numbers. Don't wait for permission; instead take ownership. Minimalism is a tool. Let it help you remove what's weighing you down and make space for life to happen.

This is about more space in your home, more breathing room to rest and enjoy and live. It's about less yelling, less stress, less fighting with your family to just clean the eff up. It's removing the need for organization, because you don't need to rearrange your junk; you need to let go of it. It's less crap in your way, less on your to-do list, and more checks on your bucket list. It's more "feel good" moments with your family.

Life is waiting to be lived. Consider how much joy and time your stuff has already stolen from you. Let the weight of that realization sink in, feel the emotions, maybe even get a little mad about it, then take action. It's time to take back your life and make your space work for you rather than against you.

LISTEN TO THE PURPOSE SHOW

How Minimalism Can Steal Your Joy

Episode 50

MON	○	TUE	○	WED	○

MON	○	TUE	○	WED	○

MON	○	TUE	○	WED	○

MON	○	TUE	○	WED	○

MON	○	TUE	○	WED	○

MONTH ....

THUR ◯	FRI ◯	SAT ◯	SUN ◯
THUR ◯	FRI ◯	SAT ◯	SUN ◯
THUR ◯	FRI ◯	SAT ◯	SUN ◯
THUR ◯	FRI ◯	SAT ◯	SUN ◯
THUR ◯	FRI ◯	SAT ◯	SUN ◯

MONDAY

....

....

....

....

....

....

◇ ....

◇ ....

◇ ....

◇ ....

◇ ....

◇ ....

TUESDAY

....

....

....

....

....

....

◇ ....

◇ ....

◇ ....

◇ ....

◇ ....

◇ ....

WEDNESDAY

....

....

....

....

....

....

◇ ....

◇ ....

◇ ....

◇ ....

◇ ....

◇ ....

◇ ....

THURSDAY

....

....

....

....

....

....

◇ ....

◇ ....

◇ ....

◇ ....

◇ ....

◇ ....

◇ ....

FRIDAY

....

....

....

....

....

....

◇ ....

◇ ....

◇ ....

◇ ....

◇ ....

◇ ....

◇ ....

SATURDAY

....

....

....

◇ ....

◇ ....

SUNDAY

....

....

....

◇ ....

◇ ....

MONDAY

....

....

....

....

....

....

◇ ....

◇ ....

◇ ....

◇ ....

◇ ....

◇ ....

TUESDAY

....

....

....

....

....

....

◇ ....

◇ ....

◇ ....

◇ ....

◇ ....

◇ ....

WEDNESDAY

....

....

....

....

....

....

◇ ....

◇ ....

◇ ....

◇ ....

◇ ....

◇ ....

◇ ....

THURSDAY

◇
◇
◇
◇
◇
◇
◇

FRIDAY

◇
◇
◇
◇
◇
◇
◇

SATURDAY

◇
◇

SUNDAY

◇
◇

MONDAY

....

....

....

....

....

....

◇ ....

◇ ....

◇ ....

◇ ....

◇ ....

◇ ....

TUESDAY

....

....

....

....

....

....

◇ ....

◇ ....

◇ ....

◇ ....

◇ ....

◇ ....

WEDNESDAY

....

....

....

....

....

....

◇ ....

◇ ....

◇ ....

◇ ....

◇ ....

◇ ....

◇ ....

THURSDAY

◇ ....

◇ ....

....

◇ ....

....

◇ ....

....

◇ ....

....

◇ ....

....

◇ ....

....

◇ ....

FRIDAY

◇ ....

....

◇ ....

....

◇ ....

....

◇ ....

....

◇ ....

....

◇ ....

....

◇ ....

....

◇ ....

SATURDAY

....

....

◇ ....

◇ ....

SUNDAY

....

....

◇ ....

◇ ....

MONDAY

....

....

....

....

....

◇ ....

◇ ....

◇ ....

◇ ....

◇ ....

◇ ....

TUESDAY

....

....

....

....

....

◇ ....

◇ ....

◇ ....

◇ ....

◇ ....

◇ ....

WEDNESDAY

....

....

....

....

....

◇ ....

◇ ....

◇ ....

◇ ....

◇ ....

◇ ....

◇ ....

THURSDAY

◇

◇

◇

◇

◇

◇

◇

FRIDAY

◇

◇

◇

◇

◇

◇

◇

SATURDAY

◇

◇

SUNDAY

◇

◇

ESTABLISH

INTENTION

MONTH

goals

TO DO LIST

- ◇
- ◇
- ◇
- ◇
- ◇
- ◇
- ◇
- ◇
- ◇
- ◇
- ◇

BIRTHDAYS

IMPORTANT DATES

reminders

AFFIRMATIONS TO STAY MOTIVATED

AFFIRMATIONS TO STAY MOTIVATED

ESTABLISH INTENTION

INSTEAD OF IMMEDIATELY PICKING UP THE FIRST THING YOU SEE, ASK yourself: What is my vision for this room? I want you to hold space for it, and really question how the room can serve you and your family. What do you need out of this space? What do you need it to do for you?

If you need some clarity, here are some questions you can ask yourself:

- Do I like how I'm using this room right now? Is it working for me?
- What do I want this room to be used for? Don't limit your answer to the traditional use for your rooms. Is there some out-of-the-box idea that you've had for this space but felt like it was too weird? You do you, girl! It's your home! Your name is on that rent or mortgage check. You can do whatever you want to make that space work for you!
- How do I want to feel when I'm in this room?
- How do I want my family to feel?
- How do I want guests to feel?
- What are some practical things I could do to this space to make it simpler, easier, and happier?
- Who am I in this room?

Your answers to these questions will lead to your intent for each space. They will determine so much of what you keep or don't keep in those rooms. We want to stop the autopilot and be intentional.

Setting the intent for each room is so important, which is why it's the first step in this journey. It will help you decide what to keep and what to move out of each space.

How to Set the Intent When It's Not Really Your Space

There are some spaces in your home that are not totally yours. For those, you'll have to work with other family members to set the intent. Places like your kid's room or a general family area like the loft or the game room. These are rooms where you're not the only person using them, so it won't feel good for everyone else if you are the only one deciding what to keep. So, how do you set the intent for these areas?

Make it a family thing! Invite family members into the decision-making process with you (if they're old enough). If it's a room your child spends time in, and they're over the age of four, ask them to help you decide how to best use the room. I've provided a list of great questions (and follow-up questions) to help get your kids' wheels turning when it comes to setting the intent for their space.

- How do you feel when you're in this room? Happy? Safe? Scared?
- Does this room make you smile?
- Do you like how this room looks right now? No? How would you like it to look?
- How would you like this room to feel? Peaceful? Fun? Calm? Exciting?
- Is there anything in here you like?
- Is there anything in here you don't like?

Ask your kids. Have the conversation. Obviously, you don't have to do anything crazy like putting in a slide (although that would be amazing). The point is to just check in with them. I think we sometimes forget that we can actually have conversations with our kids about the day-to-day things they experience. It doesn't have to be the way it's always been, and they'll appreciate that you care.

Use your adult logic here too. Do your kids have books thrown everywhere? Add a bookcase or shelves on the wall. Are you noticing anything about their room that's not lining up with who your child is? Make the space fit them more. For example, if your child is an introvert who needs time alone to recharge but there's no space for them in their room to relax and regroup, then change it.

By asking these questions, we're reconfiguring the layout of our homes and the stuff in our rooms. We're rethinking the systems that have naturally developed as we've been doing life day in and day out on autopilot. By asking whether what we've been doing is working out or not, we're taking a step back and being intentional.

IDENTIFY THE CLUTTER CRUTCH

If you're like most people, there may be a space in your home where things go to die, whether it's an entire floor, one room, or a Monica Gellar–style secret closet. It is our hidden beast. I call it the clutter crutch.

The problem with having a clutter crutch is that while you're decluttering like a mother, you always have a fallback, a safety net in which to throw things you're indecisive about. You'll just be moving your crap from one room to another, which is not progress.

The good news is, I'm not going to have you tackle that space right now. It's not the time. What's important now is being aware of the clutter crutch and promising me and yourself that whatever you do, you won't add stuff to it as you go through your other rooms. The endless, mindless cycle of throwing things in this space, adding to the monster pile, and closing the door ends right now.

LISTEN TO THE PURPOSE SHOW

Simple Doesn't Equal Small

Episode 135

MON		TUE		WED	

MON		TUE		WED	

MON		TUE		WED	

MON		TUE		WED	

MON		TUE		WED	

MONTH ....

THUR ◯	FRI ◯	SAT ◯	SUN ◯
THUR ◯	FRI ◯	SAT ◯	SUN ◯
THUR ◯	FRI ◯	SAT ◯	SUN ◯
THUR ◯	FRI ◯	SAT ◯	SUN ◯
THUR ◯	FRI ◯	SAT ◯	SUN ◯

MONDAY

TUESDAY

WEDNESDAY

THURSDAY

◇

◇

◇

◇

◇

◇

◇

FRIDAY

◇

◇

◇

◇

◇

◇

◇

SATURDAY

◇

◇

SUNDAY

◇

◇

MONDAY

....

....

....

....

....

....

◇ ....

◇ ....

◇ ....

◇ ....

◇ ....

◇ ....

TUESDAY

....

....

....

....

....

....

◇ ....

◇ ....

◇ ....

◇ ....

◇ ....

◇ ....

WEDNESDAY

....

....

....

....

....

....

◇ ....

◇ ....

◇ ....

◇ ....

◇ ....

◇ ....

◇ ....

THURSDAY

◇

◇

◇

◇

◇

◇

◇

FRIDAY

◇

◇

◇

◇

◇

◇

◇

SATURDAY

◇

◇

SUNDAY

◇

◇

MONDAY

TUESDAY

WEDNESDAY

THURSDAY

◇ ....

◇ ....

◇ ....

◇ ....

◇ ....

◇ ....

◇ ....

FRIDAY

◇ ....

◇ ....

◇ ....

◇ ....

◇ ....

◇ ....

◇ ....

SATURDAY

◇ ....

◇ ....

SUNDAY

◇ ....

◇ ....

MONDAY

....

....

....

....

....

- ◇ ....
- ◇ ....
- ◇ ....
- ◇ ....
- ◇ ....
- ◇ ....

TUESDAY

....

....

....

....

....

- ◇ ....
- ◇ ....
- ◇ ....
- ◇ ....
- ◇ ....
- ◇ ....

WEDNESDAY

....

....

....

....

....

- ◇ ....
- ◇ ....
- ◇ ....
- ◇ ....
- ◇ ....
- ◇ ....
- ◇ ....

THURSDAY

◇

◇

◇

◇

◇

◇

◇

FRIDAY

◇

◇

◇

◇

◇

◇

◇

SATURDAY

◇

◇

SUNDAY

◇

◇

MONTH

goals

TO DO LIST

- ◇ _____
- ◇ _____
- ◇ _____
- ◇ _____
- ◇ _____
- ◇ _____
- ◇ _____
- ◇ _____
- ◇ _____
- ◇ _____
- ◇ _____

BIRTHDAYS

_____

_____

_____

_____

_____

IMPORTANT DATES

_____

_____

_____

_____

reminders

ITEMS TO PURCHASE

ORGANIZATION IDEAS

HOW TO DECLUTTER
THE BATHROOM

WE'RE STARTING IN THE BATHROOM(S). THE REASON IS THIS: THE bathroom is an easy "yes or no" area. It's much easier to make decisions about old makeup and broken hair tools than about a sentimental box of valuables from your grandmother. So, by starting in the bathroom, you're setting yourself up for your most successful start.

Remember, don't try to change the way your family uses your home; just know *how* it gets used and declutter in a way that it becomes easier and more enjoyable to use.

Set the intent. In a place like the bathroom, some questions you might ask yourself to dig deeper into your intent might be:

- What do I use this room for?
- How do I want to feel when I'm in here? Or, how do I want my guests or family members to feel when they're in here?
- What are some practical things I can have in this space to make it simpler, easier to use, and happier to come into?

Maybe you'll begin to see that every space in your home has a deeper purpose than you originally realized, and that there are things you can do to serve your family, yourself, and your guests better—thus making your home a true haven!

The next step is to simply dive in. Don't get stuck in a perfection mentality before you even begin. Choose one bathroom in your house and dive in with the attitude that you're going to get done what you're able to get done. We are looking for progress over perfection. Just start!

Perfection would say: "I have to do the bathroom today. I don't know what I'm doing, but I have to do it all right now." Progress isn't about that. Simply focus for thirty minutes on getting rid of what you don't use or don't need and see what happens. Don't push yourself into a panic. Don't freak yourself out trying to be perfect. The all-or-nothing mentality is the absolute killer of productivity.

The first step in decluttering your bathroom is to clear the visual clutter. For example, if all you see when you walk into your bathroom are your kids' bath toys, that is visual clutter.

BATH TOYS

Most mamas reading this feel bad about throwing out their kids' toys, so there is often an overabundance. It feels wasteful to get rid of perfectly nice toys. Let me speak some truth to you: it is not wasteful. Keeping things you don't use is wasteful. It's wasting your time and your space and your energy.

Visualization is also a big part of making the bathroom work for you. Sure, the purpose of a bathroom is pretty functional, but how can we function well when we're overwhelmed by what we see every time we open the door?

Be brave, mama. Toss the toys. Now your kids can get in the bath, play with the few toys they actually like to play with, and easily put them away when bath time is over.

MAKEUP

Too often we hold on to items we don't use or that are way past their expiration date because we *might* use it *one day.* Or because it feels too wasteful. Or . . . we could snap out of it, realize we're not Taylor Swift and this glitter eyeshadow and hot-red lipstick isn't our look, and let it go.

Once you've thrown away all the old, expired makeup, lay out the rest of your beauty products on your counter. Take an honest look through these products and ask yourself what you actually wear every day. What do you use for your daily look? I'm not talking about makeup for a special event like a charity gala. I'm talking about products that you use on a more regular basis. What makes you up as a person when you go out somewhere? That's you. That's your look. Those are the products you keep. Maybe there's an exception, like a great red lipstick you don't use every day but like how it makes you feel, and so you have it as a special-event lip color.

You can keep that if you know you will continue to use it periodically, and it's not past its expiration date.

YOUR SECRET GROOMING OBSESSION

Every bathroom dweller has a secret grooming obsession. It's that one thing you can't not pick up when you're in Target. Mine is nail polish. A few years ago when I had a little bit of a tighter budget, I would do my own nails. But now, I get my nails done every couple of weeks by a gem of a human named Lucia. One day, I was in my bathroom going through my drawers and saw all these polishes I didn't use anymore. I realized that these were no longer a part of who I am, and I needed to let them go. I did keep the cuticle pushers and a couple of different colored polishes, so if I'm in a spot and needed to paint my own nails, I could. As I changed as a person, my space changed to match.

SHOWER

What do you use? Do you have a bunch of half-used body washes or razors? Toss them! Keep one sharp razor, one conditioner, one loofah or washcloth, and one face wash. Which one do you always reach for? That's the one you keep. Get rid of the rest. Perhaps you're budget minded and buy body wash in bulk, because you know you'll use it when you run out. That's okay. Store it under the sink or somewhere nearby but out of sight. You don't have to get rid of things unnecessarily if you know you're going to use them before they expire. The goal is to get multiples out of your line of vision.

LET'S DO IT

Now that we've gone over specific items and areas that need to be decluttered, let's start using the steps of decluttering: sort, toss, organize, put away. Normally, you won't have a donate pile for the bathroom, since most of the items have probably been used or expired, and that's not good for anybody.

When you start decluttering, you're essentially sorting things into piles. So, clear a space on your floor for making piles. Then, open a drawer and start. I'm going to remind you again: don't get stuck in perfectionism. Just open a drawer and begin by making that first decision.

If you decide to keep an item, put it in your Keep pile. If you decide to toss an item, put it in your Toss pile. If it belongs somewhere else in the house, put it in the Put Away pile. I recommend using an empty laundry basket for this last pile. That way you can throw everything in there that goes somewhere else, and when you're finished, you can carry it around to the other rooms and put items back where they belong.

Once you've cleared out the drawers and cabinets and sorted items into piles, it's time to organize the survivors. Buy some shallow baskets, cosmetic organizing trays, or anything that would make a countertop look like it's in order. I have a beautiful ceramic, circular tray on my bathroom counter that keeps a few glass jars and ointments—all herded together so they're not spread out everywhere. Also, get some bathroom totes or plastic organizers with drawers for underneath the sink.

I keep my cotton pads, Q-tips, and facial razor (I'm Cuban and over thirty—it's a problem) all in the ceramic tray on my counter I mentioned before. These are items I use every morning and night, and sometimes in between, so I want them easily accessible. What are the items that you use most often throughout the day? You'll want to keep those in an easy-to-reach spot. You don't want to be digging through the cabinets five times a day to find the things you use a lot. The key is to just keep asking yourself: *How do I function in this room?* And organize accordingly.

Last but not least, put away all the things in your Put Away pile or basket. Anything you found in this room that doesn't belong there, put it where it belongs. Then, if you have time, wipe or vacuum out the drawers or cabinets.

Remember, this is not a race. Even ten minutes at a time will help get you to the finish line. All that matters is a steady progress toward your goal of having a decluttered bathroom.

LISTEN TO THE PURPOSE SHOW

Cleaning Tips & Systems, Ft. Kendra Hennessy

Episode 33

MON	◯	TUE	◯	WED	◯

MON	◯	TUE	◯	WED	◯

MON	◯	TUE	◯	WED	◯

MON	◯	TUE	◯	WED	◯

MON	◯	TUE	◯	WED	◯

MONTH ....

THUR ◯	FRI ◯	SAT ◯	SUN ◯
THUR ◯	FRI ◯	SAT ◯	SUN ◯
THUR ◯	FRI ◯	SAT ◯	SUN ◯
THUR ◯	FRI ◯	SAT ◯	SUN ◯
THUR ◯	FRI ◯	SAT ◯	SUN ◯

MONDAY

....

....

....

....

....

....

◇ ....

◇ ....

◇ ....

◇ ....

◇ ....

◇ ....

TUESDAY

....

....

....

....

....

....

◇ ....

◇ ....

◇ ....

◇ ....

◇ ....

◇ ....

WEDNESDAY

....

....

....

....

....

....

◇ ....

◇ ....

◇ ....

◇ ....

◇ ....

◇ ....

◇ ....

THURSDAY

FRIDAY

SATURDAY

SUNDAY

MONDAY

....

....

....

....

....

◇ ....

◇ ....

◇ ....

◇ ....

◇ ....

◇ ....

TUESDAY

....

....

....

....

....

◇ ....

◇ ....

◇ ....

◇ ....

◇ ....

◇ ....

WEDNESDAY

....

....

....

....

....

◇ ....

◇ ....

◇ ....

◇ ....

◇ ....

◇ ....

◇ ....

THURSDAY

◇

◇

◇

◇

◇

◇

◇

FRIDAY

◇

◇

◇

◇

◇

◇

◇

SATURDAY

◇

◇

SUNDAY

◇

◇

MONDAY

....

....

....

....

....

◇ ....

◇ ....

◇ ....

◇ ....

◇ ....

◇ ....

TUESDAY

....

....

....

....

....

◇ ....

◇ ....

◇ ....

◇ ....

◇ ....

◇ ....

WEDNESDAY

....

....

....

....

....

◇ ....

◇ ....

◇ ....

◇ ....

◇ ....

◇ ....

◇ ....

THURSDAY

◇

◇

◇

◇

◇

◇

◇

FRIDAY

◇

◇

◇

◇

◇

◇

◇

SATURDAY

◇

◇

SUNDAY

◇

◇

MONDAY

◇ ....

◇ ....

◇ ....

◇ ....

◇ ....

◇ ....

TUESDAY

◇ ....

◇ ....

◇ ....

◇ ....

◇ ....

◇ ....

WEDNESDAY

◇ ....

◇ ....

◇ ....

◇ ....

◇ ....

◇ ....

◇ ....

THURSDAY

◇

◇

◇

◇

◇

◇

◇

FRIDAY

◇

◇

◇

◇

◇

◇

◇

SATURDAY

◇

◇

SUNDAY

◇

◇

HOW TO
DECLUTTER
CLOSETS &
SENTIMENTAL
THINGS

MONTH

goals

TO DO LIST

- ◇ _____
- ◇ _____
- ◇ _____
- ◇ _____
- ◇ _____
- ◇ _____
- ◇ _____
- ◇ _____
- ◇ _____
- ◇ _____
- ◇ _____

BIRTHDAYS

_____

_____

_____

_____

_____

IMPORTANT DATES

_____

_____

_____

_____

reminders

ITEMS TO PURCHASE

ORGANIZATION IDEAS

HOW TO DECLUTTER CLOSETS
& SENTIMENTAL THINGS

FOR NOW, WE'RE GOING TO FOCUS ON ALL THE CLOSETS IN YOUR house *except* for the ones you use as wardrobes. We'll cover those later. One small chunk of progress at a time.

If you're feeling really overwhelmed, just remember that you don't have to do it all at once. It's totally okay to commit to one ten-minute portion at a time. You have enough decisions to make as it is during your day; I don't want you to spend endless hours purging only to end up with decision fatigue that keeps you from coming back to finish what we started. So, take it slow and steady, focusing on short periods of time. You can always go back and do more later.

UTILITY AND STORAGE CLOSETS

There are so many different home layouts and so many different needs for this type of closet. The best way to figure out how to make this space work for you is to look at the gaps in your home. First, as always, set the intent. How do you want this part of your home to *feel*?

Next, do a visual scan. As you do your own scan, ask yourself these questions:

- What's littering the surfaces?
- Where are the gaps in the level of my home where this closet is located?
- What are our problem areas?
- How could I make this space work for me and my family?
- How could I turn this closet into a solution machine?

This all goes back to setting the intent in each area of your home. To set the intent for this closet (or these closets, if you have more than one), determine what the needs are in the area around the closet. The best way to figure out how a space can work for you is to become aware of what's going on around that space currently.

Once you've set your intent, start moving things out of that closet. I suggest you not pull everything out. Just get in there, pick up what's right in front of you, and make a decision: keep, toss, or donate. Make decisions, make piles, and get things out of that space one thing at a time. Slow, simple, steady progress gets the job done with the least amount of stress possible.

THE LINEN CLOSET

I receive so many messages and emails from people asking me to tell them exactly how many sets of sheets, blankets, and towels I have, because they want a magic number. Here's the problem with that kind of thinking: it takes away your power. My linen closet works for me, my number of kids, my climate, my preferences, and my laundry system. Your needs and wants are probably totally different from mine. Decide how you want things to feel, how often you're willing to do the laundry (or are already doing it), and what will work for you.

This is *your* home! You know what you need. It's okay to learn from people who are good at something. But make that something your own. You don't need a set of rules. However, I totally get that seeing what other people do is a good way to discover what might work for you. So, for my family, I have:

- Two sets of sheets per bed
- Two to four spare pillowcases (because bloody noses, boogers, and snot happen every second in my house)
- About three spare blankets for couch cuddling or added warmth
- A beach/pool towel for every person in our house (six), plus five extras for guests
- Eight bath towels for the six of us, plus two guest towels
- Two hand towels per bathroom

This is based on my family, our climate, our lifestyle, and our laundry routine.

For example, I don't go weeks between loads of laundry, so it wouldn't make sense for me to have twenty-five towels. For more information about my laundry routine, visit alliecasazza.com/laundry. When it comes to your linen closet, think about your laundry process. Not the laundry process you wish you had, or the one you're working toward, but the one you have right now in this moment. Then ask yourself how the linens in your closet can support that system.

SENTIMENTAL ITEMS

This is an area that can really trip us up because we tend to attach memories to things. Sentimentality is relative. It causes us to hold on to something because we *feel* like the item is special, not because it actually is. It's easy to attach meaning to things. The object is a visual trigger of the internal memory and the meaning you've given it.

Let's learn to honor sentimentality and be more conscientious of how we dish out that label. It might be helpful to replace the word *sentimental* with *unique* or *special*, because it really is easy to feel that everything is sentimental. Maybe a word change isn't what you need to make progress; maybe you just need to reframe the idea. Letting go of objects that have memories attached to them doesn't mean you are letting go of those memories. The memories are yours forever, no matter what is stored in your home.

One of my favorite things is to help people find *useful ways* to keep sentimental items in their home.

- Find a way to display your sentimental items.
- Put your sentimental items to use.
- Take a photo and capture your sentimental items—even letters and artwork. Then send it to the cloud or whatever form of storage system you use.

Remember, there are no rules here. If there is something extremely special to you that you want to keep but can't use in some way, then keep it. Just be careful that you don't attach memories to so many items that they bring clutter and chaos into your home. You are not your things; your things are not your memories. Your memories are within you, not within your stuff. And remember, you are allowed to go slow; it's okay to come back later and revisit what you'd like to keep and what you're ready to let go of. You will evolve in this process.

LISTEN TO THE PURPOSE SHOW

5 Things That Are Hard to Declutter (And How to Handle It)

Episode 19

MON		TUE		WED	
MON		TUE		WED	
MON		TUE		WED	
MON		TUE		WED	
MON		TUE		WED	

M O N T H

THUR	◯	FRI	◯	SAT	◯	SUN	◯
THUR	◯	FRI	◯	SAT	◯	SUN	◯
THUR	◯	FRI	◯	SAT	◯	SUN	◯
THUR	◯	FRI	◯	SAT	◯	SUN	◯
THUR	◯	FRI	◯	SAT	◯	SUN	◯

MONDAY

....

....

....

....

....

◇ ....

◇ ....

◇ ....

◇ ....

◇ ....

◇ ....

TUESDAY

....

....

....

....

....

◇ ....

◇ ....

◇ ....

◇ ....

◇ ....

◇ ....

WEDNESDAY

....

....

....

....

....

◇ ....

◇ ....

◇ ....

◇ ....

◇ ....

◇ ....

◇ ....

THURSDAY

....
....
....
....
....
....

◇ ....
◇ ....
◇ ....
◇ ....
◇ ....
◇ ....
◇ ....

FRIDAY

....
....
....
....
....
....

◇ ....
◇ ....
◇ ....
◇ ....
◇ ....
◇ ....
◇ ....

SATURDAY

....
....
◇ ....
◇ ....

SUNDAY

....
....
....
◇ ....
◇ ....

MONDAY

....

....

....

....

....

◇
....

◇
....

◇
....

◇
....

◇
....

◇
....

TUESDAY

....

....

....

....

....

◇
....

◇
....

◇
....

◇
....

◇
....

◇
....

WEDNESDAY

....

....

....

....

....

◇
....

◇
....

◇
....

◇
....

◇
....

◇
....

◇
....

THURSDAY

◇ ....

◇ ....

◇ ....

◇ ....

◇ ....

◇ ....

◇ ....

FRIDAY

◇ ....

◇ ....

◇ ....

◇ ....

◇ ....

◇ ....

◇ ....

SATURDAY

◇ ....

◇ ....

SUNDAY

◇ ....

◇ ....

MONDAY

◇
◇
◇
◇
◇
◇

TUESDAY

◇
◇
◇
◇
◇
◇

WEDNESDAY

◇
◇
◇
◇
◇
◇
◇

THURSDAY

◇ ....

◇ ....

....

◇ ....

....

◇ ....

....

◇ ....

....

◇ ....

....

◇ ....

....

◇ ....

FRIDAY

◇ ....

◇ ....

....

◇ ....

....

◇ ....

....

◇ ....

....

◇ ....

....

◇ ....

....

◇ ....

SATURDAY

....

....

◇ ....

◇ ....

SUNDAY

....

....

◇ ....

◇ ....

MONDAY

◇
◇
◇
◇
◇
◇

TUESDAY

◇
◇
◇
◇
◇
◇

WEDNESDAY

◇
◇
◇
◇
◇
◇
◇

THURSDAY

....
....
....
....
....
....

◇ ....
◇ ....
◇ ....
◇ ....
◇ ....
◇ ....
◇ ....

FRIDAY

....
....
....
....
....
....

◇ ....
◇ ....
◇ ....
◇ ....
◇ ....
◇ ....
◇ ....

SATURDAY

....
....
....
◇ ....
◇ ....

SUNDAY

....
....
....
◇ ....
◇ ....

MONTH

goals

TO DO LIST

BIRTHDAYS

- ◇
- ◇
- ◇
- ◇
- ◇
- ◇
- ◇
- ◇
- ◇
- ◇
- ◇

IMPORTANT DATES

reminders

ITEMS TO PURCHASE

ORGANIZATION IDEAS

HOW TO DECLUTTER
THE KITCHEN

YOU KNOW THE DRILL: FIRST, SET THE INTENT. I WANT YOU TO GO beyond preparing meals. The kitchen is often where people gather when you have company over. This room is where a lot of conversations take place. It's important to envision how you want to use this space, so you can set the intent and declutter the way it works for you.

Your kitchen should be set up to work with you, not against you. So, how do you cook? Do you do a lot of baking? What kinds of tools and appliances do you have in the kitchen that you use regularly? What items do you not have that would actually make your work in the kitchen more efficient? Take notes of what you see and don't like or would prefer to try a different way.

DISHES (PLATES AND BOWLS)

Take out your spare sets or partial sets and evaluate their usefulness to you. Do you host dinner parties for which you need these extra sets? Do you tend to use paper plates when company comes over? Based on your answers to these questions, decide whether to donate the dishes or store them somewhere else away from your everyday dishes.

The point is to simplify. There are a lot of ways to go about this, but they all involve simplifying. Maybe it works better for you to have more dishes and load them in the dishwasher throughout the day and then unload them in the morning. With either method, it's literally impossible to have a pile at the end of the day. Choose what works for you.

After you have streamlined and organized your dishes in a way that works for you, and you find there is a very special set that you love but rarely use and can't bring yourself to get rid of (e.g., Grandma's china or your basic whites for your holiday entertaining), pack them up in a box for safekeeping and place them in an easily accessible closet or on a shelf in the garage. You'll have peace of mind knowing they're available when you need them but stored where they won't get in the way of your everyday, functional kitchen.

SILVERWARE DRAWER AND UTENSILS

I have a drawer organizer that allows for a certain amount of space for spoons, a certain amount for forks, and so on. That's my limit. I like to keep my basic utensils (mixing spoons, spatulas, etc.) in a vase or a jar on the counter by the stove. It's easy to find one that's beautiful and looks great on your countertop!

CUPS AND MUGS

Go through your mug cabinet and quickly purge all the mugs you kind of hate. I don't know why, but we all have them. Life is too short to drink out of a fugly mug.

How's your cup situation? Mismatched? I thought so. I solved my mismatched cup situation by ditching them all and buying two cases of mason jars. They all match, they look cute when they're in use, and if I need more, I can get them at any store without worrying about having mismatched sets. Win-win.

Here's a bonus tip for those of you with little kids in the house: I love the four-ounce mason jars for kids! They even have different-colored lids for this size—and straws to fit. You could get a different color for each kid in your house, so everybody knows which cup is theirs.

POTS AND PANS

What kinds of meals do you cook? Do you use large family-size pots, or do you tend to cook small amounts in a one-quart pan? Do you *never* use a certain type of pan that you've had since your wedding? Do you have multiple skillets but always grab the same one or two? Whatever you never use needs to go, plain and simple.

Be ruthless here—pots and pans take up a lot of space. Also, if you notice some are getting scratched up and worn out, it may be time to replace them.

APPLIANCES

First things first: ditch the doubles you don't use. It's okay to have more than one thing if you have a reason and it's used. For example, I have two Crock-Pots and an Instant Pot because of my family size and the fact that we host a lot of parties. They each get used *all the time*.

Appliances are usually bulky to store. So be quite critical here when considering whether or not to keep something. Do you really use this item often enough to justify the space it takes up in your life? Is there a smaller or simpler utensil that can get the job done for you? If it's something you must keep but rarely use, and your kitchen is very tight on space, consider storing it in a lower-value real estate area of your home, like a high shelf in the pantry or even a dedicated area in a spare closet.

COUNTERTOPS

I want you to clear your counters as much as possible! Having visual white space in a room is an easy way to make it feel better. It makes the room feel more open, airy, and vibey. So let's make it happen. First, ask yourself: What appliances are used so often that it would be completely pointless and unhelpful to store them anywhere but the countertop?

If you're worried that you might not have enough space to clear your counters, try decluttering what you're not using first and then see. If you seriously lack space, that's okay; you just have to be creative. Utilize vertical space, use the space on the side of the end cabinet, look on Pinterest for creative storage solutions and spend time making them happen. I want you to enjoy being in your kitchen, and you can—it just takes a bit of intention and creativity.

Let's talk about when your counters are a catchall for non-kitchen things, such as your keys, paperwork, mail, and more. Here's my rule: where stuff collects, create a storage solution. Create a solution that supports your habits, rather than stressing out over trying to change the way you or your family members have done things for years.

So, how can we utilize this idea in the kitchen if that's where stuff tends to get dropped? Maybe it's putting a bowl on the counter for keys, hooks on a wall, or a basket by the back door. Paperwork and mail, bills, papers from school—these are big deals in the kitchen. Can you address these? Maybe you need an in-box, out-box, or to-do type of vertical organizer.

THE PANTRY

First, throw away what is expired and what is ruined. Donate what is still sealed that you know you won't eat. Then store stuff better so you can access what you're keeping.

I have a couple of simple bins for like items (cans, bagged snacks and chips, stocks, etc.) and that's pretty much it. It doesn't have to be perfect, but it does need to work with you rather than against you.

LISTEN TO THE PURPOSE SHOW

Healing Your Relationship with Food, Ft. Sarah
   Speers

Episode 225

MON	◯	TUE	◯	WED	◯

MON	◯	TUE	◯	WED	◯

MON	◯	TUE	◯	WED	◯

MON	◯	TUE	◯	WED	◯

MON	◯	TUE	◯	WED	◯

MONTH ....

THUR ◯	FRI ◯	SAT ◯	SUN ◯
THUR ◯	FRI ◯	SAT ◯	SUN ◯
THUR ◯	FRI ◯	SAT ◯	SUN ◯
THUR ◯	FRI ◯	SAT ◯	SUN ◯
THUR ◯	FRI ◯	SAT ◯	SUN ◯

MONDAY

....

....

....

....

....

....

◇ ....

◇ ....

◇ ....

◇ ....

◇ ....

◇ ....

TUESDAY

....

....

....

....

....

....

◇ ....

◇ ....

◇ ....

◇ ....

◇ ....

◇ ....

WEDNESDAY

....

....

....

....

....

....

◇ ....

◇ ....

◇ ....

◇ ....

◇ ....

◇ ....

◇ ....

THURSDAY

◇

◇

◇

◇

◇

◇

◇

FRIDAY

◇

◇

◇

◇

◇

◇

◇

SATURDAY

◇

◇

SUNDAY

◇

◇

MONDAY

TUESDAY

WEDNESDAY

THURSDAY

- ◇
- ◇
- ◇
- ◇
- ◇
- ◇
- ◇

FRIDAY

- ◇
- ◇
- ◇
- ◇
- ◇
- ◇
- ◇

SATURDAY

- ◇
- ◇

SUNDAY

- ◇
- ◇

MONDAY

....

....

....

....

....

....

◇ ....

◇ ....

◇ ....

◇ ....

◇ ....

◇ ....

TUESDAY

....

....

....

....

....

....

◇ ....

◇ ....

◇ ....

◇ ....

◇ ....

◇ ....

WEDNESDAY

....

....

....

....

....

....

◇ ....

◇ ....

◇ ....

◇ ....

◇ ....

◇ ....

◇ ....

THURSDAY

◇

◇

◇

◇

◇

◇

◇

FRIDAY

◇

◇

◇

◇

◇

◇

◇

SATURDAY

◇

◇

SUNDAY

◇

◇

MONDAY

....

....

....

....

....

....

◇ ....

◇ ....

◇ ....

◇ ....

◇ ....

◇ ....

TUESDAY

....

....

....

....

....

....

◇ ....

◇ ....

◇ ....

◇ ....

◇ ....

◇ ....

WEDNESDAY

....

....

....

....

....

....

◇ ....

◇ ....

◇ ....

◇ ....

◇ ....

◇ ....

◇ ....

THURSDAY

◇

◇

◇

◇

◇

◇

◇

FRIDAY

◇

◇

◇

◇

◇

◇

◇

SATURDAY

◇

◇

SUNDAY

◇

◇

HOW TO DECLUTTER YOUR KID'S ROOM & SPACES

MONTH

goals

TO DO LIST

BIRTHDAYS

◇ _____

◇ _____

◇ _____

◇ _____

◇ _____

◇ _____

◇ _____

IMPORTANT DATES

◇ _____

◇ _____

◇ _____

◇ _____

reminders

ITEMS TO PURCHASE

ORGANIZATION IDEAS

HOW TO DECLUTTER YOUR
KID'S ROOM & SPACES

I WANT YOU TO SET THE INTENT FOR THE CHILDHOOD THAT'S TAKING place in your home. This is sacred. It's something we often think about long before we become parents. We have goals, dreams, and aspirations of what parenthood and, in turn, our kids' childhood will look like. What often happens, though, is once we have a child, we get so busy reacting to different situations that we forget what we set out to do.

This month I want you to ask yourself: *What kind of childhood do I really want for my kids? What do I want their childhood to* feel *like?*

Getting clear on your intention for your kid's childhood will help you realize your core values in parenting, your core values as a family, and what you want to instill in that little person as they live out their childhood in your home. That intention will also help you decide what toys and items deserve a place in your home and what do not.

So, what do you want for your kids? How do you picture the rest of their childhood going? It's okay if they're not super little anymore. Start where you are. From this point on, what do you envision? How much time do you want them to spend on technology (e.g., playing video games, watching TV, listening to music, etc.)? Do you feel pretty relaxed about that, or do you really want them to spend less time using tech devices and more time outside? What climate do you live in? Is that feasible where you live? What kind of outdoor space do you have?

If you have more than one child in your house, how do you want them to interact with each other? What kind of connection do you want to help your children foster within themselves?

I believe the best way you can teach your children about wastefulness and the consumeristic society we're living in is to lead by example and include them in the process. Keep things simple. Show your kids what it looks like to remove excess, then guide them through the same process with their stuff, gently and with patience.

Children ages three and older can and should be fully involved in the process of decluttering their things. It will probably be a slower process with them involved, but this is incredibly important.

HOW TO PURGE YOUR KID'S TOYS

Here are some questions to help you bring the intent for their childhood to the physical spaces:

- What do you want for this space?
- What do you think your child wants for this space?
- How do you want it to feel?
- What function do you want it to have for your kids?
- What kind of childhood do you want to foster in your home? (Constantly revisit this answer!)
- Are the toys and clothes you have supporting that intent?

Do you see how setting that intent ahead of time makes it easier to decide what is worth keeping and what isn't?

Have a Plan

When you involve your kids in the decluttering process, it's helpful to have strategies in place and an attitude of excitement. Make a plan for what you're going to be doing so your kids can see that you're confident, you know what to do, and you're positive, not stressed. Kids pick up on your energy and emotions!

One super helpful tip I can give you here is to focus on what they're *keeping*, not on what they're taking away. It will help you and your kids if their attention is on choosing what their favorite things are, rather than what they're losing.

If they decide to donate a toy that is special to you but not to them, the best thing to do is to go with their decision. We want to encourage them in this process and empower them to make decisions.

Let's spend a moment on organization. When you organize the toys without purging, you're keeping excess stuff, and that stuff is likely going to end up dumped on the floor. Let's face it, toys do not stay organized unless Mom does it. Organization is a temporary rearrangement, not a solution.

How Many Toys Should You Keep?

I find it's much more helpful to follow this rule: have a designated space for things like toys, and when that space fills up that is your cue to purge.

You can get one big toy bin for your kids to share, or you can get one for each child. You can have several smaller bins if you want. It doesn't matter. Do what feels best for you. But do set a limit on space. The toys should not take over the house, or even an entire room, without any containment. Remember, it's not good for the kids to have too many toys to choose from.

What Toys Should You Keep?

Here are my suggestions for what to keep:

- toys that are truly cherished and beloved by your kids (the ones that cause meltdowns when they go missing)
- toys that encourage constructive play (think LEGO, train tracks, and puzzles)
- toys that encourage imaginative play (think art supplies, dress-up clothes, and books)
- toys that foster togetherness (think board games and family activities— even the iPad and gaming systems foster togetherness if people are playing together)

Also keep in mind that sometimes your kids will play with an ordinary toy in a way that's different from how it was originally intended, a way that's really creative. It's a good idea to keep toys like that!

What Toys Should You Let Go?

Here are my suggestions for what to get rid of:

- random toys like those cheap, plastic ones they give you in kids' meals

- toys and games that have key pieces missing
- toys that are no longer played with, or those you *want* your kids to play with but they don't
- large toys that are not played with often enough to be worth the space they take up, such as toy kitchens

Here are some questions to ask yourself as you're purging the toys:

- Is this toy adding to my child's life in a positive way?
- Is this toy aligning with the intent I've set for their childhood? (It always goes back to this!)
- Does my child play with this toy? (A way to check this is to ask yourself if this toy is valued and searched for when it goes missing. If not, it's really just taking up space.)

PURGING THE CLOTHES

Pull out everything that your kids haven't worn in two weeks and ask yourself (or your kids) these questions:

- Why haven't they worn this?
- Do they like it?
- Do I like it?
- Is it stained or damaged in some way?
- Does it fit or will it fit very soon?

If they haven't worn something in a couple of weeks because it's a "special occasion" item like nice clothes for an event, family dinners, church, or something similar, that's a valid reason for holding on to it. For everything else, be real with yourself about what they actually wear and why.

You also need to think about your family's lifestyle. I don't mean the lifestyle you want to have, but the one you are actually living today. Ask yourself these questions:

- What kind of family are we?
- What do we like to do?
- Are we active?
- Do we spend a lot of time outside?
- Do we go to church?
- Do we go out to dinner often?
- Do we go to a lot of nice events?
- What kind of climate do we live in?
- Do our kids often play outside and get dirty?
- Are we homebodies?
- Do we have a good laundry system?

The answers to these questions will help you determine what kind of clothes and how many you need to keep.

LISTEN TO THE PURPOSE SHOW

Why You Need to Declutter the Toys

Episode 167

MON		TUE		WED	
MON		TUE		WED	
MON		TUE		WED	
MON		TUE		WED	
MON		TUE		WED	

MONTH

THUR ◯	FRI ◯	SAT ◯	SUN ◯
THUR ◯	FRI ◯	SAT ◯	SUN ◯
THUR ◯	FRI ◯	SAT ◯	SUN ◯
THUR ◯	FRI ◯	SAT ◯	SUN ◯
THUR ◯	FRI ◯	SAT ◯	SUN ◯

MONDAY

....

....

....

....

....

....

◇ ....

◇ ....

◇ ....

◇ ....

◇ ....

◇ ....

TUESDAY

....

....

....

....

....

....

◇ ....

◇ ....

◇ ....

◇ ....

◇ ....

◇ ....

WEDNESDAY

....

....

....

....

....

....

◇ ....

◇ ....

◇ ....

◇ ....

◇ ....

◇ ....

◇ ....

THURSDAY

◇

◇

◇

◇

◇

◇

◇

FRIDAY

◇

◇

◇

◇

◇

◇

◇

SATURDAY

◇

◇

SUNDAY

◇

◇

MONDAY

....

....

....

....

....

....

◇ ....

◇ ....

◇ ....

◇ ....

◇ ....

◇ ....

TUESDAY

....

....

....

....

....

....

◇ ....

◇ ....

◇ ....

◇ ....

◇ ....

◇ ....

WEDNESDAY

....

....

....

....

....

....

◇ ....

◇ ....

◇ ....

◇ ....

◇ ....

◇ ....

◇ ....

THURSDAY

....
....
....
....
....
....
....

◇ ....
◇ ....
◇ ....
◇ ....
◇ ....
◇ ....
◇ ....

FRIDAY

....
....
....
....
....
....
....

◇ ....
◇ ....
◇ ....
◇ ....
◇ ....
◇ ....
◇ ....

SATURDAY

....
....
....
◇ ....
◇ ....

SUNDAY

....
....
....
◇ ....
◇ ....

MONDAY

....

....

....

....

....

◇ ....

◇ ....

◇ ....

◇ ....

◇ ....

◇ ....

TUESDAY

....

....

....

....

....

◇ ....

◇ ....

◇ ....

◇ ....

◇ ....

◇ ....

WEDNESDAY

....

....

....

....

....

◇ ....

◇ ....

◇ ....

◇ ....

◇ ....

◇ ....

◇ ....

THURSDAY

◇

◇

◇

◇

◇

◇

◇

FRIDAY

◇

◇

◇

◇

◇

◇

◇

SATURDAY

◇

◇

SUNDAY

◇

◇

MONDAY

....

....

....

....

....

....

◇ ....

◇ ....

◇ ....

◇ ....

◇ ....

◇ ....

TUESDAY

....

....

....

....

....

....

◇ ....

◇ ....

◇ ....

◇ ....

◇ ....

◇ ....

WEDNESDAY

....

....

....

....

....

....

◇ ....

◇ ....

◇ ....

◇ ....

◇ ....

◇ ....

◇ ....

THURSDAY

FRIDAY

SATURDAY

SUNDAY

MONTH

goals

TO DO LIST

- ◇ _____
- ◇ _____
- ◇ _____
- ◇ _____
- ◇ _____
- ◇ _____
- ◇ _____
- ◇ _____
- ◇ _____
- ◇ _____
- ◇ _____

BIRTHDAYS

_____

_____

_____

_____

_____

IMPORTANT DATES

_____

_____

_____

_____

reminders

ITEMS TO PURCHASE

ORGANIZATION IDEAS

HOW TO DECLUTTER YOUR WARDROBE

IF PUTTING OUTFITS TOGETHER IN THE MORNING ISN'T WHAT LIGHTS you up, then keep things simple. There's nothing wrong with that. But if you're like me, and you love putting your outfits together and getting dressed is one of your favorite parts of the day, there's nothing wrong with that either. Remember, don't be a minimalist for the sake of being a minimalist. Be a minimalist only where it serves you. It should be making your life *better*. If a capsule wardrobe isn't going to do that for you, then find your own version of simplicity in this area.

Even though I love clothes, have a full closet, and enjoy shopping, I don't needlessly shop. I'm not limiting myself via someone else's rules, but there's still intentionality. When I shop, I ask myself things like, *Do I already own something similar to this? What would I wear this with? When would I wear something like this?* These questions serve as a check-in that prevents me from just buying something for the sake of buying it. Everything needs to have a purpose when it enters my home.

Every single thing I own supports *my* specific body, makes me feel amazing, and helps me live out my purpose. That may sound a bit dramatic, but it's true! The things I own help me feel ready to show up as a mom, a leader, a business owner, a human being. Your closet should be doing this for you too.

I want you to go into your closet, open your dresser drawers, look at what you have, and make some decisions. If every single thing you have doesn't make you feel the way you want to feel, I want you to ask yourself why you're treating yourself that way. Why are you settling? Is it because you don't value yourself enough? Do you feel any shame or hatred toward your body? Are you overwhelmed and don't know where to buy things or where to shop for things that make you feel better? There's always an underlying reason for why we keep what doesn't feel good. The decluttering process is far more spiritual than most people realize.

As you go through your clothes, ask yourself the following questions.

QUESTION 1: DO I FEEL ABSOLUTELY AMAZING IN THIS?

This question applies to everything. Yes, even your pajamas. If you don't feel absolutely amazing in something, what's the point of owning it? If guilt comes up over the money you spent on something, remember that *it's not serving you and that's its job*. There's a lesson to be learned about valuing yourself enough to not buy things that don't help you feel amazing. Now you know, so you can shop smarter moving forward. Learn the lesson, be grateful for it, and let that item go.

QUESTION 2: WHEN WAS THE LAST TIME I WORE THIS, AND HOW DID I FEEL?

Don't ask yourself *if* you wear it or *if you will* wear it, because it's easy to lie to yourself and step pretty far out of the zone of reality this way. Rather, ask yourself to remember the last time you wore something. This forces you to come up with some amount of time, or at least a general idea.

Maybe your answer is straightforward and definitive: you wear those jogger pants all the time, but they make you feel frumpy and encourage negative body talk in your head. Toss them! Or maybe your answer is more general: you don't remember exactly when, but the last time you wore that red dress was to some event and you felt sexy, and it still fits. Keep it!

QUESTION 3: IS THIS DAMAGED AT ALL?

Don't hold on to something that has an unremovable stain just because you love it and you're bummed it got ruined. It happens. If something is damaged but it's repairable—like a rip or a missing button—then you need to get real with yourself. Are you going to have it fixed or fix it yourself? What's the plan of action?

If your plan is to repair it yourself, add a sewing kit and buttons (or whatever you need) to your shopping list, then get your phone out and set an alarm for one week from now. If your plan is to have it repaired, look up a tailor that is close to you and call to see what their hours and prices are. Then put those items in your car with a reminder to drop them off next time you're out. Setting boundaries for yourself keeps you from getting stuck.

THE HANGER TRICK

For one month, every time you wear an item of clothing, hang it back in your closet with the hanger facing the opposite way of the others. After the month is over, all the items hanging on a reverse hanger are things you wore—and likely wear the most.

Studies show most people wear 20 percent of their wardrobe 80 percent of the time.[3] This is a great way to find what makes up your 20 percent.

WHAT TO DO IF YOU DECLUTTER YOUR CLOSET AND END UP WITH NEXT TO NOTHING

I've been there. When I first cleaned out my wardrobe, I felt discouraged because I ended up with basically nothing, and I knew I couldn't afford to replace those items anytime soon. It was hard. But I stayed committed, because I knew I deserved to love my clothes and feel good in my life, no matter what my budget was. I figured it was better to have a tiny wardrobe I could mix and match, than to have a big wardrobe that didn't make me feel beautiful.

Since I had a *very* limited budget at the time (I'm talking zero wiggle room), I found ways to make an extra $20 to $40 by selling something I was decluttering or by saving money on groceries. I'd set my mind on one item I needed and invest in it as soon as I could—one piece at a time. Very slowly, I built a wardrobe I loved and that made me feel amazing.

REPLACING YOUR WARDROBE

When you're building your new wardrobe, ask yourself what is important to you. Do you want the clothes to be fair trade? Do you want them to be really good quality? Do you want the cost to be low? What is your most important priority when it comes to shopping brands?

In my experience, there are two easy ways to shop:

1. Plan a day without the kids and go to the mall or shopping center of your choice. Be prepared to try things on and make it an intentional time carved out for yourself. Don't forget to do online research before you go!
2. Order things online, try them on, and return what doesn't work. When I do this, I keep my returns in a basket by the front door, so I can go to UPS once a week rather than taking individual items as I decide not to keep them.

Another option, if you want to skip the research and just really hate shopping, is to try Stitch Fix. They do the shopping for you after you answer a few questions, then send you things to try on. You can send back anything you don't like and will only be charged for what you keep.

HOW TO STORE THE CLOTHES YOU'RE KEEPING

Ask yourself some questions to make your space work for you. Do you usually keep everything in your dresser drawers, but then everything is wrinkled when you pull it out? Maybe you should try folding things differently. Or maybe you should just hang everything. If you have the closet space, why not? There are so many tutorials online for folding clothes. Look on Pinterest or YouTube and see if you can find a way that works for you and your clothes. Get creative and find a system that serves you.

LISTEN TO THE PURPOSE SHOW

I Don't Have a Capsule Wardrobe, and
   Here's Why

Episode 5

MON	TUE	WED

MON	TUE	WED

MON	TUE	WED

MON	TUE	WED

MON	TUE	WED

MONTH ....

THUR ◯	FRI ◯	SAT ◯	SUN ◯

THUR ◯	FRI ◯	SAT ◯	SUN ◯

THUR ◯	FRI ◯	SAT ◯	SUN ◯

THUR ◯	FRI ◯	SAT ◯	SUN ◯

THUR ◯	FRI ◯	SAT ◯	SUN ◯

MONDAY

....

◇
....

....

◇
....

....

◇
....

....

◇
....

....

◇
....

....

◇
....

TUESDAY

....

◇
....

....

◇
....

....

◇
....

....

◇
....

....

◇
....

....

◇
....

WEDNESDAY

....

◇
....

....

◇
....

....

◇
....

....

◇
....

....

◇
....

....

◇
....

....

◇
....

THURSDAY

◇

◇

◇

◇

◇

◇

◇

FRIDAY

◇

◇

◇

◇

◇

◇

◇

SATURDAY

◇

◇

SUNDAY

◇

◇

MONDAY

....

....

....

....

....

....

◇ ....

◇ ....

◇ ....

◇ ....

◇ ....

◇ ....

TUESDAY

....

....

....

....

....

....

◇ ....

◇ ....

◇ ....

◇ ....

◇ ....

◇ ....

WEDNESDAY

....

....

....

....

....

....

◇ ....

◇ ....

◇ ....

◇ ....

◇ ....

◇ ....

◇ ....

THURSDAY

◇

◇

◇

◇

◇

◇

◇

FRIDAY

◇

◇

◇

◇

◇

◇

◇

SATURDAY

◇

◇

SUNDAY

◇

◇

MONDAY

....

....

....

....

....

◇ ....

◇ ....

◇ ....

◇ ....

◇ ....

◇ ....

TUESDAY

....

....

....

....

....

◇ ....

◇ ....

◇ ....

◇ ....

◇ ....

◇ ....

WEDNESDAY

....

....

....

....

....

◇ ....

◇ ....

◇ ....

◇ ....

◇ ....

◇ ....

◇ ....

THURSDAY

◇

◇

◇

◇

◇

◇

◇

FRIDAY

◇

◇

◇

◇

◇

◇

◇

SATURDAY

◇

◇

SUNDAY

◇

◇

MONDAY

◇
◇
◇
◇
◇
◇

TUESDAY

◇
◇
◇
◇
◇
◇

WEDNESDAY

◇
◇
◇
◇
◇
◇
◇

THURSDAY

◇

◇

◇

◇

◇

◇

◇

FRIDAY

◇

◇

◇

◇

◇

◇

◇

SATURDAY

◇

◇

SUNDAY

◇

◇

HOW TO

DECLUTTER

EVERYTHING

ELSE

MONTH

goals

TO DO LIST

◇ _____
◇ _____
◇ _____
◇ _____
◇ _____
◇ _____
◇ _____
◇ _____
◇ _____
◇ _____
◇ _____

BIRTHDAYS

_____

_____

_____

_____

_____

IMPORTANT DATES

_____

_____

_____

_____

_____

reminders

ITEMS TO PURCHASE

ORGANIZATION IDEAS

HOW TO
DECLUTTER EVERYTHING ELSE

MUCH OF WHAT WE'VE PURGED TOGETHER WAS THE HARD PART. IT gave you a foundation—a method to keep going—that will make other spaces much easier to work through, even if they are cluttered. Now we'll focus on the more general spaces in your home as well as any specific areas not every house has (e.g., office, homeschool area, craft room, etc.).

LIVING ROOM AND FAMILY ROOM

Time to ask the golden question: What's the intent in this space? Go stand in the room you're working on and ask yourself how you want that room to feel. How do you want it to serve your family? What's its purpose?

Sometimes when we do this, we realize the original intent of the space isn't actually what our family needs it to be. So, a living room becomes a homeschool room, or a dining room becomes Mom's office. What do *you* need from this space in your home? Decide. Get super clear. And make decisions from that clarity.

THE CLUTTER CRUTCH

The clutter crutch can be almost any space in your home: a guest room, an office space, a bedroom, a closet, a cabinet, even a piece of furniture can be used to store clutter. The clutter in a clutter crutch is always a physical manifestation of unmade decisions.

Here are a few practical tips to help you knock this out.

1. JUST DO IT. Pick it up and make a decision about it. Spend one day knocking this space out once and for all, so you'll never have to go back to it.

2. BREAK IT UP INTO A COUPLE OF SCHEDULED DAYS. Look at your calendar and block out chunks of time over two to three days for tackling the clutter crutch.

3. MAKE IT FUN. Sometimes, bringing in a fun, supportive person or playlist is all you need to finally ditch this stressor.

4. DO IT THE DLAM WAY AND SET A TIMER. There's a productivity hack called the Pomodoro Technique. Basically, you set a timer for twenty-five minutes and bust through work the entire time. When the timer goes off, you take a five-minute break. Then you go back to another twenty-five-minute jam session. You keep going until you're done.

THE GARAGE

The garage is a space in your home that could support your family and work for you. I think sometimes we forget that and treat it like an extra-large closet where we dump random stuff and things we don't want to keep inside the house.

What are the types of things you use your garage to store? How can you store those items in a way that leaves you the most space? How can you utilize vertical wall space? Do you need to buy a few bins, hooks, or shelves? What is the intent you set for this space? How does it need to work for you and your family?

Think outside the box and get creative until it's functional.

OFFICE SPACE

What's your intent for your workspace? What do you need it to do for you? How do you want to feel in here? How can you bring the energy you need to accomplish everything you do into this space through furniture, decor, and layout?

How can you infuse your workspace with this positive energy? Even if you work at the kitchen table or a small desk in the corner of your living room, this can be done with a little bit of intention. So often we buy things just because we need to fill the space, need something functional, or it's on sale, and we miss out on an opportunity to really make our space come alive and bring us joy.

HOBBY SPACES

The thing we want to watch out for is whether this space has become so overstuffed that it's no longer functional, or you avoid being in there because it's so messy. If this is the case, the room is not serving its purpose. Remove the excess. Make decisions. What needs to happen for this space to serve you well? What needs to change for you to get back to loving this activity like you once did? You're creating more time for what matters to you by decluttering it.

LISTEN TO THE PURPOSE SHOW

How to Organize Your Life When You're Not an
Organized Person

Episode 233

MON		TUE		WED	
	◯		◯		◯

MON		TUE		WED	
	◯		◯		◯

MON		TUE		WED	
	◯		◯		◯

MON		TUE		WED	
	◯		◯		◯

MON		TUE		WED	
	◯		◯		◯

MONTH ....

THUR ◯	FRI ◯	SAT ◯	SUN ◯
THUR ◯	FRI ◯	SAT ◯	SUN ◯
THUR ◯	FRI ◯	SAT ◯	SUN ◯
THUR ◯	FRI ◯	SAT ◯	SUN ◯
THUR ◯	FRI ◯	SAT ◯	SUN ◯

MONDAY

....

....

....

....

....

◇ ....

◇ ....

◇ ....

◇ ....

◇ ....

◇ ....

TUESDAY

....

....

....

....

....

◇ ....

◇ ....

◇ ....

◇ ....

◇ ....

◇ ....

WEDNESDAY

....

....

....

....

....

◇ ....

◇ ....

◇ ....

◇ ....

◇ ....

◇ ....

◇ ....

THURSDAY

◇
◇
◇
◇
◇
◇
◇

FRIDAY

◇
◇
◇
◇
◇
◇
◇

SATURDAY

◇
◇

SUNDAY

◇
◇

MONDAY

◇ ....

◇ ....

◇ ....

◇ ....

◇ ....

◇ ....

TUESDAY

◇ ....

◇ ....

◇ ....

◇ ....

◇ ....

◇ ....

WEDNESDAY

◇ ....

◇ ....

◇ ....

◇ ....

◇ ....

◇ ....

◇ ....

THURSDAY

....

....

....

....

....

....

◇ ....

◇ ....

◇ ....

◇ ....

◇ ....

◇ ....

◇ ....

FRIDAY

....

....

....

....

....

....

◇ ....

◇ ....

◇ ....

◇ ....

◇ ....

◇ ....

◇ ....

SATURDAY

....

....

....

◇ ....

◇ ....

SUNDAY

....

....

....

◇ ....

◇ ....

MONDAY

◇
◇
◇
◇
◇
◇

TUESDAY

◇
◇
◇
◇
◇
◇

WEDNESDAY

◇
◇
◇
◇
◇
◇
◇

THURSDAY

◇

◇

◇

◇

◇

◇

◇

FRIDAY

◇

◇

◇

◇

◇

◇

◇

SATURDAY

◇

◇

SUNDAY

◇

◇

MONDAY

◇ ....

◇ ....

◇ ....

◇ ....

◇ ....

◇ ....

TUESDAY

◇ ....

◇ ....

◇ ....

◇ ....

◇ ....

◇ ....

WEDNESDAY

◇ ....

◇ ....

◇ ....

◇ ....

◇ ....

◇ ....

◇ ....

THURSDAY

FRIDAY

SATURDAY

SUNDAY

MONTH

goals

TO DO LIST

BIRTHDAYS

◇ _____

◇ _____

◇ _____

◇ _____

◇ _____

◇ _____

IMPORTANT DATES

◇ _____

◇ _____

◇ _____

◇ _____

reminders

GOALS TO HELP YOU MAINTAIN

GOALS TO HELP YOU MAINTAIN

....

....

....

....

....

....

....

....

....

....

....

....

....

....

....

....

....

....

HOW TO MAINTAIN YOUR DECLUTTERED HOME

WHAT HAPPENS AFTER ALL YOUR ROOMS HAVE BEEN PURGED AND your home feels lighter? You enter maintenance mode. Decluttering is not a one-and-done kind of thing. But it's okay, because if you can get a grasp on maintaining what you did, you won't have to go back to the way things were. Like any other lifestyle change, minimalism is something you live out for good, not something you do once and then walk away from.

Keeping an eye out during day-to-day cleanup helps, but the key to keeping these random things at bay is regular maintenance purges. You can do these once a week, once a month, once a quarter, whenever you want.

THE INCOMING FLOW

Kids' school papers, birthday party favors, kids' meal toys, mail, gifts from loved ones—these are just a part of life. You want to live in a place of balance—between letting life happen and not being overly anxious about stuff—to remain the "ruthless editor" of your home.

MAIL AND PAPERWORK

Get a magazine file box. This is going to act as an "inbox" for your physical paper-work. From now on, whenever you check the mail or receive incoming papers, put them in this physical inbox.

Next, add a weekly reminder, to this planner or on your phone, to go through the physical inbox.

Every week, on the day of your choosing, you are going to sit down and deal with the papers in that physical inbox. Pay the bills, throw away the trash, look at the school flyers, take pictures of what you may need to reference again later and throw away the originals, and so on.

If something *is* urgent, you'll know when you see it in the mail; in that case, deal with it immediately instead of adding it to the inbox.

RANDOM STUFF THE KIDS BRING HOME

Kids' meal toys, party favors, those tiny toys they get as rewards—all these things and more can be filed under "random stuff the kids bring home." Here's how I handle them. Things like these are super cheap, which means they don't last. So, even if my kid is super psyched about the random little toy he got for doing great at the dentist, it's going to last about two seconds. I let my kids be kids and keep what they love.

Set a reminder in this planner or on your phone. Do you feel like weekly mainte- nance purges would be good right now? Every other week? Monthly? Pick a schedule that feels right and write it in. This doesn't need to take a ton of time. You're just checking in, moving some things out that made their way in but aren't welcome to stay.

GIFTS

Your home; your rules. Your time cleaning up; your decisions to make about what stays. Your gift; your choice.

When I have been given something I know won't get used, isn't a good fit for me, or just needs to go, I don't declutter it out of spite or annoyance. I am truly thankful to the person who gave it (I even still write thank-you notes because my mom taught me to), and I am able to let go from a place of love and gratitude. Remember, the gift is not an obligation unless you let it be. Holding on to something given to you is doing no one any favors, especially when that gift could be donated and actually used by someone else.

WHAT ABOUT SHOPPING?

The idea that living with less clutter or being a minimalist means you can't ever shop again is legalistic and pointless. That way of thinking can make you feel joyless and sad, which is the exact opposite of what we're trying to achieve.

Be a mindful shopper. Mindful shopping means having an awareness of self. It means buying things you know you'll actually use. You know exactly what you're going to wear with that sweater and which purse will match those shoes. This purchase is going to be a positive addition to your life and worthy of the space it will take up in your closet. You're not just buying something for the sake of buying it or because it was on sale. You're buying it because you need it and will use it.

LISTEN TO THE PURPOSE SHOW
Sunday Night Prep: The Key to Purposeful
   Weeks

Episode 130

MON		TUE		WED	

MON		TUE		WED	

MON		TUE		WED	

MON		TUE		WED	

MON		TUE		WED	

MONTH ....

THUR ◯	FRI ◯	SAT ◯	SUN ◯
THUR ◯	FRI ◯	SAT ◯	SUN ◯
THUR ◯	FRI ◯	SAT ◯	SUN ◯
THUR ◯	FRI ◯	SAT ◯	SUN ◯
THUR ◯	FRI ◯	SAT ◯	SUN ◯

MONDAY

....

....

....

....

....

◇ ....

◇ ....

◇ ....

◇ ....

◇ ....

◇ ....

TUESDAY

....

....

....

....

....

◇ ....

◇ ....

◇ ....

◇ ....

◇ ....

◇ ....

WEDNESDAY

....

....

....

....

....

◇ ....

◇ ....

◇ ....

◇ ....

◇ ....

◇ ....

◇ ....

THURSDAY

FRIDAY

SATURDAY

SUNDAY

MONDAY

....

....

....

....

....

◇ ....

◇ ....

◇ ....

◇ ....

◇ ....

◇ ....

TUESDAY

....

....

....

....

....

◇ ....

◇ ....

◇ ....

◇ ....

◇ ....

◇ ....

WEDNESDAY

....

....

....

....

....

◇ ....

◇ ....

◇ ....

◇ ....

◇ ....

◇ ....

◇ ....

THURSDAY

◇

◇

◇

◇

◇

◇

◇

FRIDAY

◇

◇

◇

◇

◇

◇

◇

SATURDAY

◇

◇

SUNDAY

◇

◇

MONDAY

....

....

....

....

....

....

◇ ....

◇ ....

◇ ....

◇ ....

◇ ....

◇ ....

TUESDAY

....

....

....

....

....

....

◇ ....

◇ ....

◇ ....

◇ ....

◇ ....

◇ ....

WEDNESDAY

....

....

....

....

....

....

◇ ....

◇ ....

◇ ....

◇ ....

◇ ....

◇ ....

◇ ....

THURSDAY

- ◇ ....
- ◇ ....
- ◇ ....
- ◇ ....
- ◇ ....
- ◇ ....
- ◇ ....

FRIDAY

- ◇ ....
- ◇ ....
- ◇ ....
- ◇ ....
- ◇ ....
- ◇ ....
- ◇ ....

SATURDAY

- ◇ ....
- ◇ ....

SUNDAY

- ◇ ....
- ◇ ....

MONDAY

◇

◇

◇

◇

◇

◇

TUESDAY

◇

◇

◇

◇

◇

◇

WEDNESDAY

◇

◇

◇

◇

◇

◇

◇

THURSDAY

◇

◇

◇

◇

◇

◇

◇

FRIDAY

◇

◇

◇

◇

◇

◇

◇

SATURDAY

◇

◇

SUNDAY

◇

◇

DO YOU!

MONTH

goals

TO DO LIST

◇ _____
◇ _____
◇ _____
◇ _____
◇ _____
◇ _____
◇ _____
◇ _____
◇ _____
◇ _____
◇ _____

BIRTHDAYS

_____
_____
_____
_____
_____

IMPORTANT DATES

_____
_____
_____
_____

reminders

AFFIRMATIONS TO STAY MOTIVATED

AFFIRMATIONS TO STAY MOTIVATED

DO YOU!

WHEN YOU START TO LIVE THIS WAY, PEOPLE WILL NOTICE, AND NOT everyone will like it. Some people may even push against it or seem offended by it. When you start to live this freeing, simpler yet abundant lifestyle, you're going against the norm. You're living a counterculture lifestyle. You're disrupting the flow. And the truth is, doing so can bring up some conviction in other people and they may project that onto you. The reason people react this way is based on their own insecurities and what they assume you think about their decisions. It really has nothing to do with you.

Minimalism is not about having less for the sake of having less. It's not about having a clean house. It's not about being a minimalist because it's trendy and cool and your house will look perfect. There has to be a bigger and deeper why. *It's about having less for the sake of having more of what matters.*

You are editing what is taking up space in your home, because you want to live a life aligned with your priorities. You no longer want to mindlessly allow things to pile up in your closet. You no longer want to look around at your overstuffed home and think, *This is normal. Everyone lives like this. So, I guess it's good enough for me.* No, you are practicing countercultural mindfulness for good reasons.

I've received emails from Your Uncluttered Home students who have experienced literal, life-changing results from this lifestyle shift. One woman was on the brink of an unwanted divorce. But she was able to save her marriage after implementing these changes, because she no longer created so much stress in her life, and therefore had the mental space to work on her relationship. *She created time for what mattered to her.*

Another woman shared that she felt like someone was missing from her family, but she was terrified to have another baby because of how overwhelmed she was already. After she simplified her home, she felt freer and less chronically stressed. She gave birth to a beautiful little girl whom she called "a future world changer who would not exist without this."

These stories, these changes you're making, far outweigh what others think.

When you think about it this way instead of shrinking back and asking yourself, *Is this really what I want to be doing? Is this really worth it?* you start to wonder how you can apply this to everything else in your life. You begin to think of ways to create an atmosphere of less for the sake of more in your schedule, in your job, in your relationships, in your mindset, in your health and wellness.

This effort and way of life are so worthy of your energy and so helpful that you may find you're ready to simplify everywhere. Because this works. You are aware now. You know now.

Maya Angelou said: "Do the best you can until you know better. Then when you know better, do better."

You learned, you know better, and now you can do better. You are now a part of a movement of women who are choosing mindfulness and simplicity when it comes to their homes and their families. You are leaving a legacy of intention. I'm so proud of you!

LISTEN TO THE PURPOSE SHOW

How "Enough" Lists Have Changed My Life

Episode 03

MON ◯	TUE ◯	WED ◯

MON ◯	TUE ◯	WED ◯

MON ◯	TUE ◯	WED ◯

MON ◯	TUE ◯	WED ◯

MON ◯	TUE ◯	WED ◯

MONTH ....

THUR ◯	FRI ◯	SAT ◯	SUN ◯
THUR ◯	FRI ◯	SAT ◯	SUN ◯
THUR ◯	FRI ◯	SAT ◯	SUN ◯
THUR ◯	FRI ◯	SAT ◯	SUN ◯
THUR ◯	FRI ◯	SAT ◯	SUN ◯

MONDAY

....
....
....
....
....

◇ ....
◇ ....
◇ ....
◇ ....
◇ ....
◇ ....

TUESDAY

....
....
....
....
....

◇ ....
◇ ....
◇ ....
◇ ....
◇ ....
◇ ....

WEDNESDAY

....
....
....
....
....

◇ ....
◇ ....
◇ ....
◇ ....
◇ ....
◇ ....
◇ ....

THURSDAY

◇ ....

◇ ....

◇ ....

◇ ....

◇ ....

◇ ....

◇ ....

FRIDAY

◇ ....

◇ ....

◇ ....

◇ ....

◇ ....

◇ ....

◇ ....

SATURDAY

◇ ....

◇ ....

SUNDAY

◇ ....

◇ ....

MONDAY

....

....

....

....

....

....

◇ ....

◇ ....

◇ ....

◇ ....

◇ ....

◇ ....

TUESDAY

....

....

....

....

....

....

◇ ....

◇ ....

◇ ....

◇ ....

◇ ....

◇ ....

WEDNESDAY

....

....

....

....

....

....

◇ ....

◇ ....

◇ ....

◇ ....

◇ ....

◇ ....

◇ ....

THURSDAY

....

....

....

....

....

◇ ....

◇ ....

◇ ....

◇ ....

◇ ....

◇ ....

◇ ....

FRIDAY

....

....

....

....

....

◇ ....

◇ ....

◇ ....

◇ ....

◇ ....

◇ ....

◇ ....

SATURDAY

....

....

◇ ....

◇ ....

SUNDAY

....

....

◇ ....

◇ ....

MONDAY

◇

◇

◇

◇

◇

◇

TUESDAY

◇

◇

◇

◇

◇

◇

WEDNESDAY

◇

◇

◇

◇

◇

◇

◇

THURSDAY

- ◇ ....
- ◇ ....
- ◇ ....
- ◇ ....
- ◇ ....
- ◇ ....
- ◇ ....

FRIDAY

- ◇ ....
- ◇ ....
- ◇ ....
- ◇ ....
- ◇ ....
- ◇ ....
- ◇ ....

SATURDAY

- ◇ ....
- ◇ ....

SUNDAY

- ◇ ....
- ◇ ....

MONDAY

◇

◇

◇

◇

◇

◇

TUESDAY

◇

◇

◇

◇

◇

◇

WEDNESDAY

◇

◇

◇

◇

◇

◇

◇

THURSDAY

◇
◇
◇
◇
◇
◇
◇

FRIDAY

◇
◇
◇
◇
◇
◇
◇

SATURDAY

◇
◇

SUNDAY

◇
◇

ADDRESSES

NAME & ADDRESS   EMAIL

ADDRESSES

NAME & ADDRESS

EMAIL

ADDRESSES

NAME & ADDRESS

EMAIL

ADDRESSES

NAME & ADDRESS   EMAIL

NOTES

NOTES

NOTES

1. Jack Feuer, "The Clutter Culture," *UCLA Magazine*, July 1, 2012, http://magazine.ucla.edu/features/the-clutter-culture/.
2. Marshall Goldsmith and Mark Reiter, *Triggers: Creating Behavior That Lasts—Becoming the Person You Want to Be* (New York: Crown Business, 2015), 38.
3. Ray A. Smith, "A Closet Filled with Regrets," *Wall Street Journal*, April 17, 2013, https://www.wsj.com/articles/SB10001424127887324240804578415002232186418.